SandCastle™

Baby Mammals

It's a Baby
Prairie
Dog!

Kelly Doudna

Consulting Editor, Diane Craig, M.A./Reading Specialist

ABDO
Publishing Company

Published by ABDO Publishing Company, 8000 West 78th Street, Edina, Minnesota 55439.

Printed in the United States.

Editor: Pam Price
Content Developer: Nancy Tuminelly
Cover and Interior Design and Production: Mighty Media
Photo Credits: Brand X Pictures, Getty Images (G. Richard Kettlewell), Peter Arnold Inc. (BIOS Klein & Hubert, BIOS Mafart-Renodier, C. Allan Morgan, H. Schweiger, R. Siegel)

Library of Congress Cataloging-in-Publication Data

Doudna, Kelly, 1963-
  It's a baby prairie dog! / Kelly Doudna.
    p. cm. -- (Baby mammals)
  ISBN 978-1-60453-029-2
  1. Prairie dogs--Infancy--Juvenile literature. I. Title.

  QL737.R68D68 2008
  599.36'7139--dc22
                        2007038007

SandCastle™ Level: Fluent

SandCastle™ books are created by a team of professional educators, reading specialists, and content developers around five essential components—phonemic awareness, phonics, vocabulary, text comprehension, and fluency—to assist young readers as they develop reading skills and strategies and increase their general knowledge. All books are written, reviewed, and leveled for guided reading, early reading intervention, and Accelerated Reader® programs for use in shared, guided, and independent reading and writing activities to support a balanced approach to literacy instruction. The SandCastle™ series has four levels that correspond to early literacy development. The levels are provided to help teachers and parents select appropriate books for young readers.

| **Emerging Readers** | **Beginning Readers** | **Transitional Readers** | **Fluent Readers** |
| (no flags) | (1 flag) | (2 flags) | (3 flags) |

SandCastle™ would like to hear from you. Please send us your comments and suggestions.
sandcastle@abdopublishing.com

Vital Statistics

for the Prairie Dog

BABY NAME
pup

NUMBER IN LITTER
1 to 8, average 4

WEIGHT AT BIRTH
½ ounce

AGE OF INDEPENDENCE
1 year

ADULT WEIGHT
2 to 3 pounds

LIFE EXPECTANCY
3 to 5 years

Prairie dog mothers have their pups in burrows. Pups stay underground until they are almost two months old.

Prairie dog pups are born blind and helpless.

Prairie dog mothers care for the pups. Prairie dog fathers protect their families.

Prairie dogs live in large
communities called towns.
Each town has a network
of tunnels and burrows.

Prairie dogs spend a
lot of time taking care
of their burrows.

Prairie dogs are mostly herbivores. Their diet is made up of grasses and leaves. But sometimes they eat insects.

Prairie dogs are very social animals. They interact by playing, touching, and making sounds.

Prairie dogs have a highly developed language.

Coyotes, badgers, and hawks prey on prairie dogs. But prairie dogs warn each other if a predator is approaching.

When danger has passed, a prairie dog signals with a jump-yip call. Sometimes the prairie dog falls over backward while yipping!

Female pups stay with their family groups their entire lives.

Male pups leave their families when they are one year old. They move to the outskirts of their towns.

Fun Fact
About the Prairie Dog

The largest prairie dog town ever reported was in the high plains of Texas. It was home to 400 million animals. It covered 25,000 square miles. That's an area about the size of West Virginia!

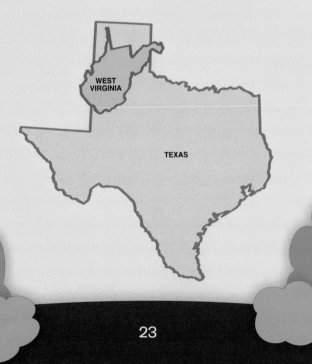

WEST VIRGINIA

TEXAS

Glossary

approach – to come near to.

burrow – a hole or tunnel dug in the ground by a small animal for use as shelter.

community – a group of animals living in the same area or having common interests.

expectancy – an expected or likely amount.

herbivore – an animal that eats mainly plants.

independence – the state of no longer needing others to care for or support you.

interact – to act on or affect one another.

network – something with parts that cross or connect, such as threads in a net, a series of tunnels, and computers joined by cables.

outskirts – the outer area that is far from the center of a city or a town.

predator – an animal that hunts others.

prey – to hunt or catch an animal for food.

To see a complete list of SandCastle™ books and other nonfiction titles from ABDO Publishing Company, visit **www.abdopublishing.com**.

8000 West 78th Street, Edina, MN 55439

800-800-1312 • 952-831-1632 fax